MINIMALIST LIVING

THE ANSWER TO FREEING UP TIME, SAVING MONEY AND REDUCING STRESS.

PAUL JUDD

D1522931

CONTENTS

INTRODUCTION

Congratulations on purchasing this book, and thank you for doing so. This book will help you understand the concept of minimalist living and how to incorporate it.

Stress, mental fog, and clutter have become regular features of our lives. We can't quite place our fingers, but we all feel that there is something that's always bothering us.

Most of us know that our lifestyles, work stress, and poor routines are responsible for most of our woes. A maximalist approach and poor control of clutter lead to these problems. That's the reason more and more people are tilting towards the concept of minimalism.

Minimalism as a concept is largely associated with keeping the clutter around us to a bare minimum. However, minimalism can help much more. It is a powerful concept that can help you eliminate several crucial problems even in your life.

Minimalist living can effectively bring down stress, indecision, and confusion in your life. It can help you lower your expenses and even make day-to-day living much easier and smoother.

Most people focus only on physical decluttering. Although that's an important part of minimalism, it can never be complete without an overall change in attitude.

Even if you get rid of the clutter once but do not change your attitude, you will again accumulate more. Minimalist living helps you eliminate clutter from all aspects of your life.

It gives you a real chance to deal with physical, mental, and emotional clutter. It doesn't just help you eliminate unwanted things but also gives you a fresh perspective on the important things in life.

Most people think that minimalism is all about removing unwanted things or decluttering. They are only partially correct. Even more than that, minimalism is about identifying important things in life and prioritizing.

We are surrounded by so much physical, mental, and emotional clutter that we can never give importance to the things where it is due. It leads to strained relationships, severed friendship bonds, and poor prioritization of responsibilities. By the time we get to realize their importance, it is already too late.

This book on minimalist living will help you understand the concept of minimalism and how you can incorporate it best in life. It will specifically focus on issues such as decision fatigue that keep you confused and strained. It will give you clear and actionable steps to deal with mental, emotional, and physical clutter.

This book will also focus on the clutter in relationships and family ties. It will help you understand the complexities and give you advice on dealing with them.

Most importantly, this book will help you walk in pursuit of real joy and happiness in your life.

Most of us keep trying to find joy and happiness in gadgets and other possessions. This pursuit is bound to end in vain. This book will help you point in the right direction so that you can feel empowered and liberated.

This book will also emphasize the things we are missing in life due to misplaced priorities. The cost of gaining all the possessions has been our simple joys. These days, we need a reason to smile. We need a reason to be joyful. That's against our true nature, where things should have been the opposite. We should need reasons to be sad; joy should come naturally.

This book will help you in understanding the things that bring joy to us and make us happy.

Our financial stability has also taken a great hit in the race to have more than everyone else or have what others have. We are in a rat race without paying attention to our needs, and our desires have grown out of proportion. We have become greedy and self-centered. This book will bring your attention to the things we are doing wrong and how to amend them. It will help you in becoming financially independent even in the limited amount of money you earn. It will show you the path to become debt-free and lead a stress-free life that can have a purpose.

It will also show you how you can have meaningful relationships in your life and share your joys and sorrows with others.

This book will help you understand life and how it can be made better by following minimalism.

There are plenty of books on this subject on the market; thanks again for choosing this one! Every effort was made to ensure it was full of useful information; please enjoy!

CHAPTER 1
UNDERSTANDING CLUTTER AND ITS IMPACT ON OUR LIVES

WHAT IS CLUTTER?

Clutter is anything that doesn't belong at a specific location at that moment. It can be an object, an emotion, or even a thought. If it is impeding your movement, progress, effectiveness, or calm, it is clutter.

Most people think that only broken, damaged, or unusable items can be characterized as clutter. It is the kind of definition that leads to the accumulation of clutter.

The textbook definition of clutter is anything that's out of place and unorganized. It covers the physical clutter, which is easy to spot. Also, it includes thoughts, emotions, feelings, fears, and aspirations that can make lives equally chaotic.

Most of the confusion, incoherency, and chaos we see in and around us emerges from clutter. Clutter is an umbrella term that can carry a lot of things. People like to define clutter in their unique ways. What may be an asset for one can be a clutter for others.

There should be clarity in definition when it comes to clutter.

Anything that doesn't belong at that specific location is clutter.

Stop making exceptions if you want your life to be easy. The more exceptions you add to the rule, the harder it would become for you to get hold of your place and even your life.

This rule doesn't just apply to physical stuff. It applies to people, thoughts, and emotions.

- A limiting thought just before you are going to give an important presentation is clutter
- A prejudice against someone or something when you are going to make an important decision is clutter
- A book sitting untouched on your dining table for a few days is clutter
- Even the thought of your wife nagging you about something while you have to pay attention to your boss is clutter

Out of place objects, thoughts, emotions, fears, and apprehensions are forms of clutter. All can be equally damaging. It is essential to understand the damage each kind of clutter can cause and prevent it.

RAMIFICATIONS OF CLUTTER ON OUR LIVES

Clutter is obstructionist. Irrespective of the nature of the clutter, it will hinder movement, progress, or development.

. . .

Physical Clutter

Suppose you are getting ready to leave for work and open the wardrobe full of clothes. You stand perplexed. You have to decide what to wear. You stand there looking for a better choice.

Now, you must remember:

- You bought all those clothes
- All of them looked good on you, that's why you bought them in the first place
- What stares at you isn't a choice; it is indecision

It is just a simple example of clutter we have in and around our lives that remains hidden in plain sight. That wardrobe has always been there. We face the same indecision almost daily. Yet, most of us never care to do anything about it.

A few affected by the indecision simply conclude that whatever they have in the closet isn't any good, and they add a little more to it. Hence, the next day, they have a few more to choose from.

Physical clutter may look like an asset, but more often than not, it is a liability. It drains your time, energy, finances, and focus.

Mental Clutter

Mental clutter is even more troublesome. Most of us start the day with one or another remorse:

- Some people repent the lack of joy in their lives
- A few regret the beginning of the day because they got up late
- Most fret that they'd have to labor through the same mundane routine
- A majority keep nursing the hangover of the leftover thoughts of the previous day

What we don't realize is that these simple thoughts are also a part of mental clutter. They are obstructionists. They impede the way into a new and vibrant day that could have a million possibilities.

Most of us wake up feeling unhappy and disgruntled over something or the other. Even if not, we don't find a reason to be happy. Is that really so.

Can you imagine that 150,000 people lose their lives every day? That's right, these many unfortunate people will not be able to see the sunrise you have the privilege to. Now, think of the immediate family members, close friends, and dependents. Every individual has 10-15 such people. It means this morning wouldn't be the same for at least a million people.

- Don't you think that an absence of adversity is also a reason for joy?
- Don't you think a reason to feel fortunate is that you and your loved ones are healthy and fine?
- Don't you think our minds should focus on finding sources of joy rather than reasons for gloom?

Unhappiness and discontent have become the flavor of the season. Nobody seems to be content. There seems to be a more profound longing for something indiscernible. Yet, people are unable to place their fingers on it.

It happens because the clutter prohibits you from looking at things clearly in an organized fashion. You are looking at too many things at the same time, and they are blocking clear perspective.

You have too many things running in your mind at the same time. It takes away the space for clarity. It's like atoms firing from all directions. Hitting a correct idea is nothing more than a chance.

If you have started thinking that dealing with mental clutter is tough, dealing with emotional clutter is a different ball game altogether.

Emotional Clutter
Emotional clutter is the hardest to identify. One will have to be very mindful to discern clutter from valuable thoughts and emotions. We have more than 50,000 thoughts a day. Most of these are running in our subconscious brain. They have the backing of our memories, feelings, fears, hopes, aspirations, and apprehensions. What we may think of as a valid emotion can be a fearful thought. It can impair our perception and decision-making abilities.

Suppose you are going to deliver a presentation to some important clients. However, you've had a bad experience with these clients earlier. Another presentation with the same bunch would make you conscious and fearful. Fear is the primary emotion. Fear doesn't come alone. It is supported by several secondary emotions like anxiety, worry, sadness, disappointment, and discouragement.

There is no reason for the second presentation to go like the first. It depends on how you prepare. But, the fear within you starts working up the secondary emotions. That's the emotional clutter you carry at the back of the mind. As the time of presentation comes near, you start feeling more and more conscious. Even prejudice about clients may also arise in your mind. There is no substance to all this. But it doesn't even need to be. It is all emotional clutter working you up from within.

Even before you know it, the feelings of exhaustion, loss, and utter disappointment take over.

Most of us like to think that we run things around us. However, that may not be the case. Our thoughts, behaviors, choices, impulses, words, and actions are reactionary. All of us, except little toddlers with no retention power, act as vacuum cleaners. We swoop everything around and use the experiences, emotions, and feelings as reference points.

AVOSKA- THE PERHAPS BAG

The term Avoska has always intrigued me. Literally, this Russian word describes anything shapeless, oversized, or untidy. However, that's not what it was used for.

In the former USSR, Avoska was used for a simple string bag. Something easy to fit in ladies' handbags and men's pockets. Whenever needed, it could easily be unfolded to carry groceries.

. . .

'Avos,' the root of the word, means' perhaps or maybe' in Russian. Usually, it was never carried to get something specific. People always had it on them because any grocery item available at the stores could be carried in this. It was a symbol of the desperation of the ordinary Russian people of that time.

- Avoska didn't represent need or choice
- It represented gloom, desperation, and hopelessness

The scarcity of things was pretty standard in the lives of ordinary folks of the erstwhile USSR. They usually didn't get too many things at the grocery stores then and didn't even know when they could get those things. In fact, getting most of the provisions was a thing of chance.

So that was the justification of the Russians for keeping an Avoska in their pockets at all times. It seemed that the bag didn't signify desires but whatever you could lay your hands on.

The availability of things was so scarce that they wouldn't hesitate to pick even those things they didn't need immediately. They feared that they might not get those things in the future when needed. This paranoia became the second nature of people.

WHY HAVE WE BECOME SO DESPERATE TO PICK ANYTHING WE CAN LAY OUR HANDS-ON?

It seems that the people of the so-called developed and prosperous west always carry that imaginary Avoska at all times.

There are only three significant differences:

1. There is no scarcity
2. There is no real need
3. There is no conscious decision making

The question above may look abrupt and demeaning, but it is the most appropriate question for self-introspection.

Avoska was one of the eccentricities of Soviet Russia. Ironically, that purposeless bag had a profound purpose there.

But, what can be the justifications for developed and prosperous western societies to demonstrate such snatch and grab mentality?

- Don't we seem eager to pick every feeling, thought, or object we can lay our hands on?
- Has it occurred to you that a seemingly harmless conversation with your co-worker kept you awake at night?
- Do you fear politics and infighting at your workplace?
- Do you feel dissatisfaction in your life?
- Do you feel there should be something more exciting?
- Aren't we becoming 'Avoska' people with a similar snatch and grab mindset?

Have you wondered lately:

. . .

We don't buy things because we need them; we do so because we feel we should.

- Usually, it leads to clutter in homes. The average American household has more than 300,000 items. According to National Association for Productivity and Organizing Professionals (NAPO), 80% of the items we keep at our homes are never or rarely used.

We don't say things because we need to; we do so because we feel we should

- There are no reasons for forcing our opinion on others, yet we do that. A Pew Research Center survey found that 64% of Americans feel that unnecessary activism on social media negatively influences lives. On the false pretext of awareness and information, people mostly peddle misinformation, made-up news, harassment, hate, extremism, negativity, and sensationalism. In the garb of freedom of speech and expression, we are snatching the peace of mind of others. We try to force our ideas on them.

We like social media platforms for making new friends. It is an accessible medium to connect and interact with people. Yet, we have a poor friend retention rate and an even poorer close friend ratio.

- A Pew Research Center study states that an average

American adult has 634 ties in the overall social network but a little over two discussion confidants.

Usually, we don't react to things; we overreact and have meltdowns

- The beginning of the coronavirus pandemic scared people so much that they bought toilet paper worth $12 billion. That's more than the GDP of Mozambique, a country of more than 31 million people. Of all the things in the world, toilet paper. Really!!

These aren't random facts but instances from our lives' physical, mental, and emotional aspects. We all share parts of these things. These are issues that plague all of us.

Modern society, in general, isn't suffering from scarcity; it suffers from:

- Decision fatigue
- Insatiable itch to:
- Have a little more
- Say little more
- Be visible a little more
- Be heard a little more
- A little more than we possess
- Inefficient utilization of things at its disposal

People usually like to believe that these quirks and idiosyncrasies are unique to them. Sadly, these aren't.

DECLUTTERING ISN'T EASY BUT CERTAINLY REWARDING

Most people are trying to find easy ways to declutter things. Whether it is decluttering physical stuff or the mental and emotional stuff, decluttering would always be challenging. That's a fact. The sooner you come to terms with it, the better.

However, decluttering is very rewarding. You feel content and relieved after you get rid of the clutter around you. Think of something you always wanted to let off your chest and the moment you did so. Such actions may have consequences, but they can always take away the burden.

The same is the case with physical clutter. A place with too many things crammed in too little space is always distracting. There is no peace of mind at such a place. However, getting rid of things isn't easy. Most of the things are bought with money. So, it hurts to throw them away like that. Then you also have a fear what if you need them in future.

If they were given by someone, then they'd have sentimental or emotional value.

Discarding such things is even more difficult. It is how physical clutter accumulates.

There can be no easy way to get rid of clutter. Irrespective of the nature of clutter, decluttering is always going to be difficult.

The bigger problem than that is the reaccumulation of clutter. You can't be serious in thinking that just because you were somehow able to get rid of it the first time, you wouldn't accumulate it again.

Hoarding is a habit. We carry that invisible avoska with us. It is always trying to bypass our prudence. That's where minimalism comes. It is the way out of this perpetual clutter collection habit.

MINIMALISM ISN'T A GOAL BUT A NECESSITY

Minimalism is an uncomplicated way to get rid of clutter. It can help you keep the clutter out of your life. When I said an uncomplicated way, I didn't mean easy. It simply saves you from the most emotionally challenging decisions by taking away choices from you.

In simple words, minimalism is an idea of living life with only the essentials. Most people associate minimalism only with fewer possessions. However, that's not correct. Minimalism is a broader concept that also helps you manage your thought and emotions.

Minimalism is an approach to conscious living. You stop accumulating things that don't mean much to you. Objects, thoughts, or emotions; you only keep whatever is essential. Minimalism is the art of letting go of unwanted, unnecessary, and unhelpful things.

When people talk of the minimalist approach or minimalist living, they are mostly talking about decluttering.

You also need to understand that decluttering is a technique. There can be several ways to declutter. Minimalism is a way of life.

. . .

Decluttering can be learned, and there can be many ways to declutter. However, minimalism is a way of life, and you need to incorporate its principles into your life.

Minimalism as a concept looks very alluring to many people. It is so liberating that people start thinking it to be the end. In reality, it isn't. Happiness, joy, and satisfaction are the end goals we are trying to achieve; minimalism is only a means to achieve them.

Therefore, when we talk about minimalism, we are not talking about any technique. That also makes it a bit difficult to learn and incorporate.

There are no shortcuts and more accessible ways into minimalism. Everyone has to follow the same path of shredding things to the bare minimum.

However, you always have a choice. Minimalism for a monk would mean stripping off all the material and worldly possessions. Most monks even leave their families and relations. An ordinary individual doesn't need to follow that path.

You can simply try:

- Learn not to hoard things
- Learn to survive only with the essentials
- Learn better management of thoughts and emotions
- Learn not to allow your thoughts and emotions to control you
- Learn to live with joy and satisfaction

Most importantly, you must understand that minimalism is not the end goal. The end goal is to have a fulfilling and purposeful life.

If you are immersed in the rat race of life, you can never be on the quest to your true calling. You will always have the task of accumulating money for the next purchase and finding the place to put it. Then you'll want to show it to others and then again get on the task of impressing others with other, more significant, better possessions. This race is neverending; sadly, life is.

Minimalism is your way out of this rat race on to a personal quest. It is a journey to find joy and satisfaction. The beginning will always be rough because you'll have to address some of the most challenging questions in your life. You will have to address the issues you have been brushing under the carpet, but the result is always more satisfying.

CLUTTER- THE REAL HANDICAP

Clutter is usually seen as a visual handicap. Many people feel crippled by excessive bombarding of thoughts and overpowering emotions. However, it is even more potent than that. Clutter can affect your social and personal behavior, your thinking pattern, and your health. This book will help you understand the real implications of clutter on our life and decision-making abilities and how to deal with them.

CHAPTER 2
A MAXIMALIST APPROACH-
THE WRONG TURN

WHAT IS MAXIMALISM?

Maximalism is a tendency to find joy in more. Maximalism in art and design means adding more colors, textures, and patterns to make the design rich. It is a style of giving weight to the design by filling it up.

Maximalism in life means a desire to have more. Maximalism is an idea with no outer boundaries. To a greater extent, it is the cause of most of our worries.

Maximalism pushes us into the rat race. Growing up, we're told the more, the merrier. If you have one car, it's good, you have more than one, it is better. A big problem with this approach is that there is no finish line. Once you get into the rat race, there is no end to it. No matter how hard you run, you can never be declared victorious.

. . .

Our ancestors began their journey as maximalists. All the conquests, empires, and expansions in history prove that conclusively.

Maximalism isn't a bad idea as long as it is followed in pursuit of knowledge. It helps in the betterment of society. However, once maximalist tendencies get reflected in material pursuits, they never help.

To a great extent, Alexander conquered the known world of his time. Yet:

- What did he gain?
- What did he contribute?
- What could he take with himself?
- What could he enjoy?
- Could you conclusively say that his life was of joy?

Possessions do not mean joy. They can contribute to your joys to an extent, but they can't give you joy. If money and possessions could give you real joy, the cases of substance abuse, alcoholism, and other eccentricities wouldn't have been so high in the rich and the famous. When you are in pain, no worldly possession makes you happy. The heart wants what it wants.

YOU CAN SUFFER ABUNDANCE

Most people may find it hard to believe, but you can also suffer abundance.

Excess of anything is bad. More money doesn't mean more joy in life. People can also suffer from having more fame, prestige, and choices. Everything has its burden. That's the reason you'll find the richest people in the world behaving frugally.

While everyone may not have similar resources, we do have our fair share of possessions and attachments. These possessions, attachments, and desire to have more can lead to an inexplicable amount of suffering.

The biggest problem with material abundance is that it leads to vices and distraction. The desire to have more affects our satisfaction levels, lifestyles, mindset, psyche, and attitude.

The desire to have more becomes so overpowering that you become immune to what you have. Your possessions lose all value to you. The biggest problem with this mindset is that there is no outer limit. You can never have everything to yourself.

Hence, the richest man in the world is also not sitting at ease. A person earning billions is also working hard to make more or maintain that money.

That's the problem with abundance. It makes you a slave. It doesn't allow you to relax and enjoy what you have. It doesn't permit you to throw the towel and forget everything else to live life on your own terms. You will always remain conscious of what others are doing, thinking, and talking.

DECISION FATIGUE- THE AFTEREFFECT OF MAXIMALISM

If anything has plagued the developed and prosperous the most, it is decision fatigue. From early in the morning, you are bound

to make countless decisions. Some decisions require active partic-
ipation. They are important and productive decisions. However,
most decisions are useless and unproductive decisions. You have
to make them because you have a mess around yourself, and you
have no way out without making all those decisions.

For instance:

- Selecting the clothes to wear for the day
- Deciding where to go for lunch and what to eat
- Should you work on this project or that
- Should you first finish this project or take a short break
- Would a short social media break between work hurt
- Whether to buy a 40 or 55 inch Tv
- Whether to buy more coffee mugs or not
- Whether to buy that new shirt or not
- Whether to go for that movie or not
- Whether to talk to your co-worker or not
- Whether to speak to your boss or not

These are useless decisions that you shouldn't have to make most
of the waking hours of your day. These are unproductive. Most
importantly, they make you feel exhausted, defeated, overly
conscious, and guilty.

Everything you leave or buy starts a new train of doubtful
thoughts. Any decision you do not make will have some consequences, and they'll keep bothering you. If you left the 55 inch Tv
due to financial constraints, your mind would keep worrying
about the benefits of having it. It will drain away all the joy of
having this 40 inch Tv as well. The same happens with most
decisions.

.   .   .

When you have to make so many decisions, you overtax your mind. It leads to decision fatigue. Some scientists also call it ego depletion. On average, we take anywhere between 10,000 to 40,000 decisions in a day. That's a huge number. Suppose most of these decisions are useless/unworthy decisions. In that case, there will be no power left to make meaningful decisions leading to greater problems.

Have you noticed that by the end of the day, the agility of your mind goes down? You feel less inclined to participate. An interesting study in Israeli courts revealed that judges were more inclined to give parole to convicts who appeared in the morning than those who appeared later in the day. The percentage difference was stark. 70% of the prisoners appearing before the judges in the morning got parole. In contrast, only 10% of the prisoners appearing in the evening got parole.

The study concluded that constant decision-making by the end of the day made the judges more conscious of their decisions. They denied parole to remain safe or not to take unwanted risks.

Has it occurred to you that when you tried to shop anything online but ended up wasting hours and buying something different than what you initially was searching for? You went shopping for something essential within your budget but bought something much more expensive.

You went to your boss to complain about some extra task but returned with more work on your back.

It happens with most of us most of the time. It happens because we are never able to determine the full extent of our needs and desires. Hence, it becomes easier for others to convince and lead us.

. . .

If you think that decision fatigue has nothing to do with a maximalist attitude, you are wrong. The tendency to have too many things on our plate is something we have picked since our formative years. We see such dilemmas to be a part of choice.

We get habitual of making so many decisions that we don't mind the burden of making a few more decisions. However, it doesn't pass away without consequences.

Decision Fatigue Affects Our Decision-Making Abilities

A 2014 study published in the Journal of American Medical Association (JAMA) had some interesting inputs. It reflected on the decision of the doctors to prescribe antibiotics with the time of the day. It established that clinicians in the US were 26% more likely to prescribe unnecessary antibiotics in the fourth work hour of the day.

You might have noticed that most people shy away from making smaller decisions. No one wants to choose the restaurant if there is someone else to choose. The same goes for food and clothes. The reason for this is simple, the brain gets so tired of making inconsequential decisions, it wants to delegate the responsibility.

However, we can't delegate most of the decisions. Many decisions aren't even inconsequential. However, suppose the mind is tired of making decisions. In that case, it will treat even the important decisions with similar clarity and alertness. That's how the risk of making wrong decisions in life increases.

While most people never even think of maximalism and the resultant decision fatigue, it has the power to put us in a great mess. The misery most of us feel in our lives can be attributed to this decision fatigue to a great extent.

You may think that everything in your home is there because you need it. However, a quick audit of the things you haven't used in the past year, six months, three months, and a fortnight would bring much clarity.

We don't usually buy things because we need them. We buy them because they were presented to us and we were made to feel that they were important. Do you know that every day an average American sees more than 10,000 advertisements? Our subconscious records everything and keeps triggering us to have more. The longing to have that which isn't yours is a conscious effort. Producers and marketing companies earn this way.

The Curious Case of Decoy Pricing: Have you ever wondered about the price difference between various popcorn buckets at movie theaters? Have you noticed that while the difference in price between a medium and a small may be huge, the difference between the price of a medium and large bucket is very small? Do you know this is intentional?

It is called decoy pricing. The prices are arranged so that the consumer feels more inclined to buy a larger bucket. The same is the case with other pricing schemes like buy one get one free. The consumerist market wants to sell you more. It wants you to consume more.

Decision Fatigue Eats Into Our Time

The time wasted in making decisions is the time wasted. Hours and hours wasted on online marketplaces like Amazon are never going to come back. People waste hours trying to find a sweet deal that could save them a few bucks. However, they undermine the costs incurred on the additional products they pick on the way and the cost of their own time wasted in the pursuit.

We waste several hours in a day thinking about doing something while the time required to do those things isn't even minutes. From social media platforms to useless emails, we waste hours in a day. Most of it can be attributed to decision fatigue.

Decision Fatigue Affects Our Satisfaction Levels
Another crucial impact of decision fatigue is on our satisfaction levels. When we aren't making conscious decisions or forced to make too many decisions with variables, the satisfaction level in such decisions is very low.

Suppose you are trying to think of a place to go out for lunch. Now there can be no straightforward answer to this question. If there is no fixed routine, going to any of the restaurants is justified. Because there is no definite answer, the satisfaction level from the answer would be minimal.

Our routines are such that we have to make several such decisions in a day. They not only eat away our time, but they also provide very little satisfaction. This discontent can grow rapidly and make us feel discontent in general.

Therefore, while maximalism may look like a perfect lifestyle choice, it isn't. This capitalist, consumerist, market-oriented lifestyle can leave you feeling utterly dissatisfied.

. . .

Decision fatigue not only leads to dissatisfaction it also adds to stress. People start feeling stressed about simple choices like where to go out or what color to wear for the party. These aren't the kind of choices that should ever bother you. They are inconsequential.

LEARN TO DEAL WITH DECISION FATIGUE

Most decisions do not need your active involvement. However, even some simple decisions can cost you a lot of time and cause stress. A quick glance at an online sale can cost you an hour. Making the choice of breakfast can be tough for some people. To sleep or to go for a walk can be a harassing dilemma. These decisions can cause decision fatigue. They can make you feel exhausted, spent, or numb.

The best way to avoid facing decision fatigue is to follow some simple steps:

Build Habits into Your Schedule
Bringing habits into your schedule is the best way to avoid such decision-making points. If you have a fixed schedule that you follow, then such worries wouldn't arise. Fix a time for daily activities. Following a schedule keeps you sharp and makes you more efficient. It also eliminates the chances of procrastination in your life.

Be Firm About Your Choices
The dilemma of whether you are choosing the best or not can be crunching. However, most of the time, it is a baseless debate. If there is a product, it is made for the consumption of someone. Do not look for the best qualities in the products, look for the qualities that you desire and once you find them, stick to your decision. Indecisive people radiate a lot of negativity.

. . .

Make Joy and Happiness the Parameter for Your Decisions

The final deciding parameter of most of the things should be the amount of joy it would bring in life. We all have this as the end goal behind all our decisions. However, mostly this is hidden behind riders. If I buy a bigger TV than John, I would have an edge, and that would make me happy. This is a bad decision process. John can buy an even bigger TV at any point, and then my same TV would start making me feel miserable. If you are going to buy a TV, then the only correct question is the kind of TV that would make you really happy. The kind of viewing experience you would want. The amount of clarity you are looking for. The size that would fit your wall and suit your room size. Your joy and happiness should be directly behind your decisions and not some hidden agenda. It would take away the decision fatigue.

Choose a Role Model

Following a role model is always easy when you are picking such habits. It makes your choices simple. If you have a role model, then put them in your place for easy and stress-free decision making. Imitating their decisions will absolve you of all the responsibility and fatigue. The ultimate goal of the practice is to ensure that you have to make fewer such decisions on a daily basis.

You do not have to lose your identity. It is only for making decisions that have no effect on the course of your life. In fact, an easy decision-making process frees up a lot of time for you. You will be in a better position to ponder over the larger problems in a relaxed manner.

Learn to Say 'No'

Being resolute is very important for the success of any such exercise. Despite your efforts, there will be times when you'll be standing at the crossroads. You'll have to learn to firmly make a decision and go with it. You may not have the clarity, but if you keep fighting with the idea, it will lead to stress. Learn to live by your decisions.

Some Simple Stress Saving Habits

Eating Similar Food

Food is an important choice that we make every day. You have several meals a day. If you start spending 10-15 minutes before every meal to decide the menu, you are doing a great disservice to yourself and humanity. You are only useful for the food-producing industry. The best way to expedite the process, or to make it simple, is to either plan in advance for the week or month or eat similar food daily. You can have minute variations but stick to the same script. This will save a lot of time and effort.

Have a Smaller Wardrobe

Trim your wardrobe as much as possible. The lower the number of choices in clothes you have, the shorter you'll take to get ready. It will save time, and you wouldn't have to ponder about your shining armor daily. Limited choice of clothes is a strategy adopted by some of the most successful people in the world.

Follow Daily Routines

Follow daily routines like clockwork. If you are being lenient about your routines, then you are cheating yourself. Stick to the routines as they help in the formation of rigid habits. Look at the people retiring from military service. They need to train daily in the morning for around two decades. It is a compulsion in the beginning. But, they find it hard to shun the habit even after they have retired. The routine becomes a part of their life. It keeps them fit and function.

Have Fixed Corners in Your Schedule

Do not compromise with the time of separate activities. Everything has definite importance in life. If you have designated a specific time of the day for one activity, do not try to fit the other into it. This adjustment trains your mind to make a compromise. It also has to make an unnecessary decision. Strictly avoid it in all circumstances.

If something makes you Feel Anxious, drop it

Do not do things that cause stress. Modern life mandates us to do several things under peer pressure. This is tiring and uninspiring. If you do not like anything, learn to stay away from it. It will cause unnecessary levels of stress and anxiety, which you had been trying to avoid in the first place.

Do not fall into the trap of Problem of Choice

Economists say that the biggest problem of this world is not poverty or hunger; it is a problem of choice. Rich or poor, man or woman, healthy or sick, we all have to face this problem. We have to make numerous decisions on a daily basis. Some decisions make you feel liberated, and others crush you down. The marketing industry has perfected the art of using the problem of choice to its advantage. They put you in the trap of choosing between better and worse, small and big, cheap and costly, bright or dull, light or heavy, and in the process, you end up making choices that were not even required. Keep your choices simple if you want to remain happy and stress-free for the whole of your life.

CHAPTER 3
THE CONCEPT OF MINIMALISM – WHAT IT ENTAILS

Simplistic living or better known as minimalist living isn't anything new. This concept that involves getting rid of all your clutter and stuff has been a thing for a long time. If you do some research, you will find that throughout history, many religions have lived this way for many thousands of years. Take Buddhism for example, they are told to "shun all material possessions." But this practice did not become popular until the 1900s when architects, beatniks, photographers, writers, and artists started embracing this idea. The *New York Times* states that this movement started with the art community.

With that being said, as with any movement, the minimalist living has changed with the times. Due to Marie Kondo inventing tiny houses, this practice is becoming popular once again. People all over the world are seeing that less can truly be more. Here is all you need to know about learning to live a minimalist life and this includes the benefits of bringing order into you life.

THE MEANING OF MINIMALISM IS VERY SELF-EXPLANATORY

Even though the meaning of minimalist living is going to mean something different for everybody, Caleb Backe thinks that every minimalist will share some common goals. Caleb is a certified wellness and health expert at Maple Holistics. Being a minimalist means that the person will intentionally focus on the things that truly matter to them. Some people are going to believe that they have to get rid of anything that won't make them happy. If something doesn't "spark joy" in your life you need to get rid of it. What you have to realize is that possessions are just part of the entire picture.

If you want to live a minimalist life, you have to intentionally choose to have less possessions. While it might be easy for you to keep your life and home free of clutter, your social calendar might not look that way. If you can apply the same concepts to your social calendar, you might be able to find joy doing fewer things. You will have a lot more free time to do what you really love and be around the people that mean something to you.

Biggest Benefit Is Time

There are many advantages to living a minimalist life. Having less clutter means you won't have to spend as much time organizing or cleaning your home. You will have more time for your friends and family. Living a minimalist life lets you focus on what means the most to you. If you can keep an environment that is free of clutter, you will be able to increase your productivity and focus and this will reduce your stress levels. This increase won't just be psychological. One study done in 2009 found that clutter could increase your cortisol levels. Cortisol is the stress hormone. This means if you can free your house from all the things you don't need, it could help free your mind.

· · ·

Then There's Money

A minimalist life can also have some wonderful impacts on your bank account. You will have more money because you will be more careful with what you buy, especially the things you need instead of the things you want. You create wellness when you get joy from saving money and not just spending it.

HOW TO BEGIN A MINIMALIST LIFE

The first thing you need to do to start a minimalist life is to closely look at all the things and people you associate with. When you start looking at the objects in your life, you need to ask yourself three things:

1. Do you need it?
2. Do you love it?
3. Do you use it?

If the item in question doesn't strike passion or purpose in your life, it doesn't need to have a place in your life but this application is a lot easier said than it is to do it.

Begin small. Start with a list of cons and pros if you have to. If you can't decide on if you want to keep an object or not, place it to the side. Decluttering will get a lot easier the more you do it.

You need to surround yourself with the people who bring you joy, support you, challenge you, and encourage you. Minimalist living is all about having just a few things.

You will find that some things are easier to get rid of than others. If you have some family members that are toxic, it might be hard to go your separate ways. If this is the case, you have to set some boundaries. Having a detached contact is about being able to be present physically but stop being wounded emotionally by other family member's actions. Do your best to stop any and all attempts to get you to get involved with drama or an argument.

Minimalist Checklist

Even though there are certain things that any minimalist needs like bedding, food, and clothes. What you have in your home is going to be different for everyone. The best things about being a minimalist is it is going to look different for each person. A photographer is going to need some items that a teacher doesn't.

While a minimalist lifestyle won't ever be a "one size fits all," the main goal for anyone is to keep the items that you have that bring purpose and meaning to you. You have to continuously ask yourself: "I know I want this, but do I really need it?"

Once you start a minimalist life, you need to practice it each day. Why would you waste time getting rid of all the things and people in your life if you just fill it up agains with junk and clutter? You can create a routine and start a journal.

When you make the decision to become a minimalist, it is an external and internal process. Begin some type of gratitude journal or make a list of the things you would like to achieve and begin checking those things off of the list. You need to take a look at your routine and find any parts in your daily life that you could change to help lighten the load.

It is very important that you make your schedule as simple as possible, stop saying yes to obligations that you can avoid just because you feel guilty when you say no. Tell someone yes only if you really want to or if you have to in order not to lose your job.

There are going to be some tasks that you are going to have to do, and there are meetings that you are going to have to attend. You can't just ghost your boss just because you want to, but you can prioritize yourself and your well-being.

It might be as simple as cutting your makeup routine in half or reading a book rather than mindlessly scrolling through your phone while eating breakfast, figuring out which parts of your day can be made more simple, and changing your routine accordingly.

THINGS YOU SHOULDN'T DO AND WHAT YOU NEED TO DO

You want to become a minimalist, but you just aren't sure how to get started. No need to worry; every minimalist out there has been in your shoes. It can be extremely overwhelming to get started. You might be excited because you know that minimalist living can change your life, but where in the world can you start?

If you are a workaholic or even a shopaholic, your life is probably one big cluster of a mess. You are already bust and just thinking about trying to declutter your life seems impossible and overwhelming.

That sounds about right, doesn't it?

If this sounds like you, keep reading. I have been a minimalist for more than ten years now, and I have learned quite a bit. Here are some of my best resources and tips to get you started on your minimalist journey.

Let's begin by talking about some things that you shouldn't do when you begin your minimalist journey. These are some mistakes that I have seen people make. I am including them not to judge anyone because I have done these things, too.

I just want to save you money, energy, and time so that you can have the best start. For some people, it might take them years to finally decide to become a minimalist and make the changes needed.

I want you to do better than me, and this brings me to the first item:

- Stop Procrastinating

There are two reasons why a person puts off beginning their new lifestyle. One, they have problems committing to living a minimalist life since they don't know the "rules." The main thing that kept me from starting this lifestyle was thinking that it had to be "all or nothing." There really is just one rule when living a minimalist life: you have to be intentional about the things you bring into your life.

The main goal of living a minimalist life is to line up your relationships, commitments, and physical things with what matters the most to you. If you are honest with yourself about the things that bring joy and value to your life, then you are on the right track to becoming a minimalist.

The next reason a person might struggle with in getting started with this lifestyle is they don't think they have the time to do it. Most people want to know how to be a minimalist since their lives are cluttered and busy. You have to realize that you can't change your habits or lifestyle overnight. There isn't any shame in beginning with tiny steps. You aren't going to be able to declutter your whole house in a few days.

You can easily begin by lessening what you bring into your life. This just might be the easiest way to begin your minimalist life, and it will save you money and time.

The best advice I can give you on becoming a minimalist is to just do it. Do one thing to get you moving toward your goal.

- "One Last Shop Syndrome"

You have finally decided you want to be a minimalist, and you are ready to begin; there could be one thing that stands in your way, and that is "one last shop syndrome." This is similar to eating everything in your house before you begin a diet. You think you are ready to begin a minimalist life, but you just HAVE to get a few more things.

The first thing about living with less shouldn't be purchasing more. The main concept of minimalism is having quality rather than quantity. You can't decide to begin with replacing or upgrading your things. You have to be comfortable with needing and owning less.

Keep in mind if you are a perfectionist, this can sabotage your efforts. Even if you don't, perfectionism has a way of sneaking in and taking over just to get you to procrastinate. There will never be the perfect pair of sneakers, the perfect black trousers, or the perfect suit. You would be better off putting your energy into loving what you have already.

- You Don't Get Rid of Your Stuff the Right Way

You have to have a plan on what you are going to do with the stuff you are getting rid of before you begin decluttering. If you just start filling boxes and bags with the things you don't want, you are going to get overwhelmed about what you need to do with this stuff. You might end up just doing nothing and those boxes and bags are going to sit in a spare room or your garage forever.

This is going to put a stop to your enthusiasm. The best thing I can tell you to do is either have a garage sale the day after you clean things out and what doesn't sell, take it to a local charity. If you find things that are broken or beyond repair, throw them in the garbage. When you are looking for a charity, do some research and find a place that aligns with your beliefs. This can help with making sure things reach the right people who need it.

If you can have a plan as to what to do with the things you get rid of before you begin decluttering, you will follow through with the plans you made, and you won't have numerous bags of stuff all over your house. This might feel like a lot more work; it will be well worth it. It will make you stop and think about what you are bringing into your life.

- Don't Make It About "Stuff"

I know we've talked a lot about decluttering, and this is because many people will focus on this when they will begin their new lifestyle. It is very easy to get excited about decluttering, and it is easy to judge yourself by how many trash bags and boxes you have filled up and taken to charity. But what you have to understand is being a minimalist isn't about decluttering, just like living a healthy lifestyle isn't all about dieting.

Yes, decluttering is part of minimalism, but if you quit there, you are totally missing the point. Owning a lot of stuff is normally a symptom of a larger problem that should be addressed. If you just declutter without talking about the other problems, it will be easy for you to just go out and buy more things. This is the equivalent of doing yo-yo diets.

You have to realize that owning less stuff isn't the main goal. Minimalism should be a tool to help you make the life you will love living. Getting rid of stuff that don't mean anything to you can help you have more space, energy, money, and time to do the things you love.

This basically means creating a minimalist mindset and doing inner work which is as important as cleaning out your closet. Remember to ask yourself: What am I making all this space for? What do I want out of life? What values do I have? If you are able to answer these, you will learn the total benefits of being a minimalist.

- Judging Others and Yourself

When you begin your minimalist lifestyle, the first thing you have to get rid of is judgment. You have to stop judging other people and yourself. Let's begin with yourself. Decluttering can be hard since it means you have to face numerous mistakes. You might realize that you have wasted so much money of some things that you might not even use. This could be extremely painful and it might make you give up before you even get started.

You have to learn how to use self-kindness to your benefit. You have to let go of any angriness you feel toward yourself and learn how to look at your mistakes as things we can learn from. This can make a huge difference in the way you approach not only your decluttering but your general life.

You also have to stop judging other people. There will be a time where you will actually get to the minimalist lifestyle. You have downsized everything, and you begin to mindfully think about your life. This is when you are tempted to judge others.

This probably won't be intentional, and sometimes you are excited about the ways your life has changed, and you just can't figure out why everybody isn't doing the same things you are doing.

. . .

Whether or not it is intentional, judging others isn't productive or kind, especially if you have been trying to get your friends and family to live a minimalist life, too. You need to just be an advocate for the minimalist lifestyle by living your best life. You have to allow other people to learn ways to be a minimalist by just watching what you do. Never judge, only inspire. Never preach, only encourage.

CHAPTER 4
PRIME OBJECTIVES OF MINIMALIST LIVING

"*Have nothing in your houses that you do not know to be useful or believe to be beautiful.*" – *William Morris*

I would hazard a guess that most everybody reading this right now has lived the majority of their life in a cluttered home. You have closets packed to the brim, dresser drawers that refused to close, things stuck everywhere, and unfinished projects all over the place. If you know you had guests coming, you probably cleaned like crazy so that the house looked presentable. The issue with cluttered homes isn't that the people living in them don't notice it or don't care. In fact, it has more to do with the fact that they can never get ahead of the mess.

How would you like to have a house that is pretty much free from clutter and rests in a state of order? In this section, we will go over a system that can help you do just that. It doesn't even matter how far from clutter-free your home is.

Believe it can happen: The first thing you need to do in getting your home clutter-free is to believe that it's possible. Most of us already believe this to be possible, which is likely what brought you here in the first place. You are looking for a bit more guidance to reach that goal of a clutter-free life.

There are still some that aren't so sure, though. They have lived most of their life in a cluttered home and have given up hope of living any other way. The first thing you have to do to declutter your home is to believe in your heart that it is possible to do so. Know that you can't reach that goal if you don't decide in your mind that you can do it. So find that glimmer of hope you need, and take that first step. Then take another step, and another.

Get rid of the excess: Homes tend to be full of things. Clutter starts to show up when we own too much. The fewer items a person owns, the easier it becomes to keep the clutter down. The first thing you need to do to remove clutter is to get rid of your excess possessions that are taking away your energy, lives, and time.

When it comes to removing the excess, it's helpful to figure out what your definition of clutter is. Clutter can be seen as too much stuff for the size of the area. It could also be anything that you no longer love or use. It might even be anything that creates a feeling of disorganization. You can also define it by all three, and with that as a guiding filter, you can move from room to room, getting rid of everything that fits that explanation.

There will be times when this is easy, such as:

- Junk drawers that have a bunch of junk like old keys, rubber bands, and dead batteries.
- Closets that have a bunch of clothes that you haven't worn in months.
- Decorations that are outdated or no longer meaningful.

Then there will be times when it will take more time to figure out, such as:

- Large projects like the attic, garage, or basement areas.

- Sentimental items that you have picked up over your lifetime.
- Books.
- Clutter from other family members that have started to invade common areas.

The biggest player in finishing this step is to begin with the smaller and easier projects. As you work through these small victories, you will gain more motivation for the harder cases of clutter. If, by the time you finish the smaller ones, you still don't feel capable of removing excess possessions elsewhere, gain some encouragement with an intermediate step. This could mean placing the things you can't quite throw out into a box that is out of sight and writing a date on it. In a few months' time, go back through that box. While getting rid of unnecessary things is important, it isn't a race.

Start habits that manage clutter: Maintaining clutter in your home isn't just about organizing, cleaning, and then more organizing. For the most part, people struggle with maintaining clutter because they didn't take the time to remove the excess in some fashion. When the excess is still present, it doesn't matter what you do; you just can't get ahead. This prevents healthy clutter-clearing habits from emerging. So make sure you follow the second step; it is the most important part of this process. The more energy you invest in removing the excess, the easier it becomes to create habits to manage your home.

After the excess is gone, you can find which habits can keep your living space clutter-free. Once you have gotten to experience the freedom of living a clutter-free life, you will find that it's easier to embrace those habits.

Some of these habits will happen every day:

- Cleaning up the kitchen after cooking.
- Put daily-use items up once you are done with them.
- Finishing projects around your house.

- Coming up with an evening routine.

Some habits will be about a certain location that acts as a clutter collection site for the home. Kitchen counters often collect a lot of items, like schoolwork and mail. The living room will often see more traffic, and there will likely be a bedroom that is just a bit messier than others. These areas will need more effort to keep in order.

Some of your habits will have seasonal needs:

- Changing things out as the season's change.
- Getting rid of excessive possessions after birthdays or holidays.
- Big changes in life will require adjustment and refocusing.

Clutter tends to attract clutter. Once it starts to build up, it will require intentional action to get rid of it. You will need to come up with habits that work for you to help manage your daily clutter. Once you know what needs to happen, the easier it will be to implement.

Slow the accumulation of items: Living means you will consume. You can't avoid this, especially in our culture and society. However, you do have the power to slow the influx of possessions into your home to help manage clutter more efficiently.

To help slow your accumulation of things, you have to change your mindset and evaluate your purchases in a different manner. Remember that each purchase costs more than just the price. Each item will require effort, energy, and time once they come into your home. Before you make a purchase, start by answering these questions:

- Do you really need the item?
- Do I have a place for the item once I get it home?

- How much work with this bring into my life?
- Am I purchasing this for a good reason?

This isn't about keeping you from buying things every again. Instead, these questions are supposed to help bring more intentionality into your life. They will bring you more awareness to the purchases you make and what they can offer your life. It will help to slow how much you bring into your home. It is possible to have a clutter-free home.

MINIMALISM WITH FAMILY

Living a minimalist life is possible even with a family. Being minimalist doesn't mean having everything neat and organized all of the time. It means you focus on quality over quantity, and sometimes the house gets messy, but you know what to do to get it back in order.

When it comes to minimalism with your family, you have to figure out what things add to your family's life. From there, you can avoid the things that will take away from that. This mindset can change everything. How can you make that happen? Think about these two things:

- Get clear on the things that your family values.
- Figure out what gets in the way of that.

Your kids will be more willing to get involved when they think it's a fun family project and not simply "getting rid of stuff."

First, get real about what's really important. You can't skip this step. This is what will make or break your minimalist life with your family. Here's a quick set of questions that your family should answer together.

1. What do you do together that doesn't bring value into your life? What would you like to do less of?

2. Come up with a chore you hate. Is there something you could do to get rid of that chore?

3. If you had to leave your house with just a backpack, what would you put in that backpack?

4. After you have minimized your life, what will you maximize? Think about family experiences and vacations. What would you do as a family if you didn't have as many chores and more money?

Put the answer to these questions in a place in the house where everybody can see it. This will work as a reminder and a motivator. Let me reiterate, you must do this as a family. What your children say should have just as much weight as what you and your spouse say.

The second step is to remove time wasters. To take the time to sort through and declutter your home will require you to make more time for those tasks. You are going to have to look at your schedule and figure out where you can fit these things in if you are really going to commit to this. Take a look at what you spend time doing, and see if there is a way to cut back and carve out some more time. Things you should look at are:

- Television time
- Toy cleanup
- Clothing

You can schedule time to watch television so that you aren't wasting your day away watching TV. You can also help your kids go through their toys and get rid of what they don't play with. In the US, most kids have upwards of 200 toys and only play with 12. Then go through everybody's clothing and get rid of what they don't wear. This will get rid of space and time wasters, which will clear up a lot in your house

Keeping a home clutter-free can be fairly easy when you live alone. When it comes to doing so with a family, you are going to have to schedule that time in. Schedule in time each week for sorting through items.

The best way to get your children involved in all of this is to lead by example. Don't start throwing their things out without their input. That's going to cause problems. Show them how to get rid of stuff by getting rid of things you don't need or use. Let them see you do what you want them to do.

MANAGING THE CLUTTER OF WORK

The average person will spend a third of their life at work, which is why it's important to know how to bring your minimalist lifestyle to the office. When you take a minimalist approach to work, it can get rid of distractions so that you can focus on getting your job done.

Much like keeping a clutter-free home, you can keep your desk at work clutter-free and minimal. The great thing about most workspaces is that it is uniquely yours. Most of the time, other people don't use your desk at work, so you can set it up however you like. What can you do to keep your clutter at work minimal?

Question everything: One of the best things you can do is to question everything. The most dangerous thing you can say in the office space, and life, is, "That's the way it's always been." Having this mentality will prevent you from changing, growing, and improving. When you have employees or a company that can't change or improve, they tend to be the first ones to go out of business or lose their jobs.

This doesn't even apply to physical items you keep on your desk, but the work that you do. I had a friend who got a new job, and when the person leaving the position was training them, they asked why on everything. Of course, the previous employee defended each step, but my friend took notes and continued to question everything. After being trained, they went over everything with their boss. About 25% of everything caused the boss to say, "Oh, I didn't know that was still being done. We no longer need that step." They were able to eliminate about 25% of the steps they had been trained to do.

They also went and spoke with their co-workers who they would be sending reports, and most of them said they didn't use them, so they eliminated that as well. Then they got clear on what needed to be in the reports that were used, and most of the fields had changed or been eliminated.

By the time they got settled into their new job, about half of the work that the previous person had been doing wasn't needed. They were able to reduce more work later on by asking questions.

Go paperless: A big clutter causer in the office is paper. Luckily, more offices are going paperless, which makes workspaces easier to organize. So take a look at the paper on your desk and then ask why it is there.

As you go through the paper pile, you will likely notice that each document will fall into one these categories:

- It's old and should be thrown out.
- It is finished and needs to be filed away.
- It's waiting on somebody else to finish it up.
- It's waiting for you to complete it.

An interesting thing about humans, especially when trying to get rid of things, is that we like to jump to the hardest task, then convince ourselves it isn't going to work. We do a great job at talking ourselves out of doing something before it ever starts.

Schedule some time to sort through paperwork and then throw away the stuff that needs to be gotten rid of. Then move onto the paperwork that is completed but will have to be filed away or dealt with in a manner other than throwing it away. If you know what to do with papers, then it is less likely that they will pile up.

You can scan a lot of your paperwork into the computer.

There are printers that will scan paperwork and send it to you as a PDF in an email. This can help save time and remove clutter.

Then you have the documents you don't know what to do with. This is often where decluttering tends to fall apart. You have to come up with a way to deal with these questions so that your process doesn't fall apart.

Continue to scan all of your paperwork in to the computer and place the files you don't know what to do with into a separate folder. For the paperwork that requires something from somebody else, all you have to do is follow up with the other person.

Eliminate, automate, and outsource: When you start questioning things, you will start to see your workload free up. When it comes to assessing your work clutter, the first thing you need to do is eliminate it. Of the things that can't be eliminated, what can you automate and then look at the things that can be outsourced to somebody else?

Eliminating something gets rid of the task entirely, which will free you of your energy and time. Automation means that you set up something in a streamlined or automatic process that will get rid of distractions. Automation isn't the first step because it will take time to set up the process. You should always eliminate a task if it's not needed before you start to set up an automated process.

Lastly, you can take any other jobs that you don't have to do yourself and ask somebody else to do them. This should always be the last step.

Create a system: Systems help you to meet goals. It will create order and reduce your decision-making process. A system is simply a way that you will approach a task. Start out by looking at your biggest daily task. Making progress on this will have bigger impact. Write down the steps you take to finish that task. Then look at which steps can be eliminated, and then look through to see what can be automated. Go from there to work on creating the things you need to automate the process. Then look at what can be outsourced to others.

When it comes to creating systems, you will want to have bullet journals, checklists, and tracking sheets to ensure everything is getting done when it is supposed to be. Trello is a great project management software to use for this.

Manage your time better: If you aren't great at managing your time, then you'll have to pay for the consequences. Whatever time management tool works for you, use it. Schedule time for your tasks, breaks, lunch, relaxation time, meetings, and everything else you want to do. Once you have gotten a grasp on managing your time, you will be better at defending it as well. Once you have your schedule set, stick to it. There will be distractions that will try to pull you away. Find ways to remove those distractions.

Sometimes you will also have to say no and set boundaries with co-workers. We all want to come off as friendly and agreeable, but saying yes to everything is not helpful. With co-workers, saying no will be hard at first, but it will get easier. When it comes to your boss, it can be tricky. The best thing to do is make it a bit painful if they don't like respecting your time. When your boss asks you to do something, you can say, "I'm working on this project for you. If I switch to something different, the delivery date on this will have to be pushed back. Which is more important?" This will help to show the consequences of adding last-minute tasks.

TACKLING MENTAL CLUTTER

Living a minimalist life isn't all about getting rid of physical clutter. It also has to do with getting rid of mental clutter. Life can get overwhelming, which can make our minds get noisy. How can you deal with all of that?

Some days mental clutter can be worse than others. It could

be something happening now or something from your past popping back up in your mind. When you take the time to deal with the various areas of your life, it can help to cut down on the mental clutter.

The first thing to look at is your health. The mind and body aren't living in separate corners. A person who is physically unhealthy often has a poor mental state. The brain is a very delicate organ, and you need to treat it as such. Have you ever noticed that your mind races more when you are hungry or haven't slept well? Once you notice those correlations, you can start to tackle them to remove the mental clutter.

Then you can look at your circumstances. It can be difficult to look at your circumstances and think, I can change those. However, if you want to get rid of your mental clutter, then you don't have a choice but to change your circumstances. You may need to cut out certain people from your life, downsize your possessions, and change your spending habits.

You need to start with yourself, and eventually, your circumstances will change. You don't have to let circumstances change you. These changes can be difficult, but they can make you feel better in the long run.

Next, take the time to look at your past. We will all make mistakes, let people down, and make dumb decisions. However, there is no need to beat yourself up over this. Guess what? It doesn't matter how often you play those through your mind; you can't change what happened. So, when you start to feel anxiety over previous experiences, try asking yourself these questions:

- Is this a relevant situation?
- Was that even all that serious?
- Is this being blown out of proportion?
- Was I in complete control of that situation?
- Does what that person said have validity, or are they acting out?

This can help you figure out what matters the most and what doesn't. This can help you stop being so hard on yourself. It will also help you figure out what is in your control and what isn't. If there is something that isn't in your control, you have to learn how to accept it and focus on the things you do have control over.

Lastly, figure out what makes you tick. One way to do this is to take a piece of paper and draw a vertical line down the middle. On the left, write "bad days," and on the right, write "good days." List out the things that tend to cause you to have bad days and then the things that make your days good. Once you have an idea of what you like, then you can start guiding your life towards something that will make all of your days good.

CHAPTER 5

IDENTIFYING AND UNDERSTANDING THE PRIORITIES IN LIFE

P riorities can help you find your purpose in life. Losing sight of what your priorities are can lead to a lot of uncertainty. Priorities can also help when it comes to living a minimalist life.

A textbook definition of priorities is that it implies something that is your main concern. The simplest way to put it is that priorities are the most important things to you. Moreover, how do these priorities benefit you? Of course, paying bills would be a big priority because if they aren't paid, then you would lose important resources. However, priorities go a lot further than basic responsibilities.

SORTING YOUR PRIORITIES

The first thing you have to do when it comes to sorting your priorities is, to be honest with yourself. When you come up with unrealistic goals, it ends up being counterproductive. When you have priorities that you are more likely to accomplish it will lead you towards more success.

- What things do you need to do?
- What is most important to you?

This is where you need to think about *wanting* something and your *need* for something. Ensuring that your bills are paid is something that needs to happen. These needs are considered priorities. When coming up with your priorities, you will need to list out the needs in your life and mark them as such.

Once those things have been met, you can start to work towards meeting your wants. Not only will this help you feel accomplished, but when you reach your wants after taking care of your needs, it gives you a sense of completion.

Once you are honest with yourself about your priorities, you can take the time to make a list. While this may come off as tedious, lists can help to put things in perspective. They give you a chance to be more honest about what your goals are, and it will help you to know if your priorities are right. The list will act like a foundation that you can grow upon.

Let's go over some ways to help set your priorities.

- Come up with a list

As I've already said, coming up with a list of priorities can help you to keep things in perspective. Physically writing them out is best, but you can also use a digital list. Either way, a list is very helpful. This list will likely stay fairly consistent. While some things can change, there are some priorities that will remain the same.

- Figure out necessary over non-necessary

It can seem hard to figure out which tasks are necessary and which aren't, but it really isn't. Look over your list of priorities and figure out which ones are the most important and urgent. You need to place the tasks that are the most important and urgent at the top of your list. For tasks that are a personal priority but aren't urgent, they would go further down on the list

- Don't overwhelm yourself

It can be easy to feel overwhelmed. Some deep breaths and looking at your list can help. The key to ensuring your list stays manageable is being honest and realistic about what's on the list but keeping it simple as well. The list shouldn't be extremely long. If you have a long list, then you are likely trying to accomplish too much. Part of being honest with yourself about what is on your list is to know what things you can and are willing to complete.

- Know that you may need to compromise

Compromise is not easy. This is especially true when it comes to priorities that you hold dear to yourself. Remember that priorities can change. Compromise is necessary. You may experience roadblocks that can set you back. You shouldn't discourage yourself. Instead, you should look for a compromise.

- Look at your most productive days

A great way to set priorities is to utilize the days of the week where you know that you tend to be the most productive. The days you have off from work tend to be go-to days for most. However, that's not necessarily the best course of action. It can be overwhelming to spend all of your days off working on your priorities. Instead, pick one day a week where you work to tackle as many priorities as you can tends to be the better approach.

- Come up with a timeline

Your priorities will need a timeline. You also need to be realistic about your priorities. When you set too many at once, it can become unrealistic. Coming up with a timeline will help to alleviate stress and pressure. Feeling rushed will only amplify your list. Some people do well under pressure, but there are a lot of us who can't. When you have a mapped-out timeline of how you will approach your priorities, it can help reduce those feelings of being rushed.

Everybody will have different priorities. Priorities are things that we all will have to tackle. With life, it can sometimes seem hard to get these things in order, but if you follow these steps, it can make it just a bit easier.

MAKE CONSCIOUS CHOICES

To make a wise decision will require two things. One, consciously reducing how much choice that has to be made. Two, practicing intentional choosing.

Consciously reducing how many choices have to be made and routinizing the decisions can be done through minimalism. For example, figure out ahead of time what you are going to eat and wear during the work week, when you will exercise, and what types of self-care you are going to use during the week. This will help you to better prioritize your decision making process, especially when you are faced with something challenging. This will allow you to enjoy new experiences because you will have more energy and time to appreciate them.

To lower how many decisions you have to make during the day, you can take a minute each morning to reflect on what choices you would like to focus on that day. Try to be as specific as possible. Of course, there will be urgent and unexpected things that may require your attention. But when you are clear on how you want to approach the day, it will help you to stay on track. Having a less cluttered mind can help you be more responsive.

Do you prefer things over experiences? Notice if you spend a lot of energy on shiny, bright objects instead of actions that will help enrich your life. Those objects are things that will compel you, but they are ultimately empty because they won't enrich you. Being distracted by shiny objects could mean that you have a hard time making decisions. Try to focus within yourself and not outside of yourself.

When you use skillful decision-making, all of those endless options won't be a distraction anymore. Prioritize the decisions that line up with your aspirations and values. You have to be willing to take risks in your decision-making for the sake of the things that are most important to you.

HAPPINESS IS A CHOICE

Everybody is looking for different ways to be happy. Self-help books and podcasts talk about it all the time. It has become the main topic in conferences and at Ted Talks. Everyone wants to BE happy, but nobody has ever been able to find it. Why? Because being happy is a choice. You can't just BE happy; you have to choose happiness.

. . .

So, how do we choose happiness? This is an ethical decision. It is just like choosing to be angry or sad. Just because you decide to be happy, it doesn't mean you will feel happy immediately. It can take many steps.

Look at this example: you find yourself in a situation where your natural reaction is to be upset or angry, but you stop and change your reaction. You realize you don't want to stoop to another person's level, and this is great because you are totally aware of the way you are reacting and how you are feeling.

It is fine to be sad or angry for some time, but you decide to work through it until you feel happy. You have the choice to stop dwelling on it. This is the epitome of choosing happiness. Please note that even though we are talking about this, understand that everything isn't written in white and black.

It is totally impossible to feel happy in all situations. It is fine to experience emotions, even negative ones, every now and then. We have to seize every opportunity to take the high road when we can. There might be times when this choice isn't possible, and that is fine. It just makes the times of deciding to be happy worth it more.

How can happiness be a choice? Even though happiness is a choice, it can be a hard choice for some people if you look at the science of it. People who suffer from depression or anxiety might experience problems choosing to be happy in certain situations compared to a person without these conditions.

This isn't saying that it will be totally impossible, but they have to work harder at it. This is very mentally exhausting, so they have to be forgiven for their actions. This helps teach us that we can't always "judge a book by its cover."

Ways You Can Choose Happiness

- The Way You React In Situations

It isn't about the things that happen to us in life but the way we react to them. Just think about someone who is always happy. Most of them have faced extreme adversities like having their appearance damaged, a loved one dying, or battling a disease like cancer, but they still choose to be happy. Look at all the things happening to you and react so that you find peace.

- Choose The People Around You

You are the sum of the five people who you are around the most. You might find that some of these people are toxic, and it won't matter if they are family or friends. It could be time for you to sit down and talk to them about the way they affect your life. You need to try to work out a plan for the relationship.

If they don't or won't cooperate, you can tell them nicely that you have to protect your energy if they don't want to compromise. Many people aren't going to like this but it might be necessary for your real happiness.

- Pick Activities That Show The Real You

What you do outside of work or school and your hobbies need to show you who you really are. These activities also need to be enjoyable. It might be volunteering at a local food pantry, a soup kitchen, or an animal shelter. You might start hiking, playing your favorite sport again, or taking an exotic cooking class. Find things that resonate with the real you and build on those things.

- Smile

It takes a lot more muscles to frown than it does to smile. Even in moments when you aren't feeling well, just try to smile. It has been shown to release endorphins that make you feel good, and it could help you "fake it til you make it."

- Look At The Glass As Being Half Full

The main factor in being happy is optimism. Deciding to look at the bright side in any situation could help you be happy. Happy people have a tendency to find all the good things about any situation, and it won't matter how hard or tedious it might look on the outside.

- Embrace Change

Change is going to happen whether or not we want it to. There are two kinds of people in the world: people who are bitter and hate change and the ones who embrace change and adapt. Yes, change isn't always comfortable. There isn't one person in this world who likes change but change can be good. Think about what our society would be now if we didn't progress beyond the caveman.

- Honor and Take Care of Your Body

Making some small changes like drinking more water, moving more, and eating healthier could make a world of difference. You aren't just going to feel better, which could lead to happiness, but you are going to look better. Your skin will start glowing, you are going to be stronger, and you are going to have more confidence.

- Do the Right Things

Deciding to do the right things in certain situations can be hard. When everything is said and done, knowing you did the right thing could help your conscience. Having a track record of deciding to do what is right will give you some righteousness, and this will, in turn, bring you happiness.

- Love

Most people haven't experienced love from other people, and these people are very broken. It is wonderful what deciding to be happy, and some small acts of kindness do for others. It doesn't just make them feel good, but it will make you feel great, too.

- Become One With Nature

Getting outside in nature for 15 minutes each day has been proven to improve a person's happiness. At lunch, sit outside and let the sun shine on your face. This gives you a good dose of Vitamin D that most people are deficient in. Getting out in nature can have a meditative and calming effect on you. Seeing some wild animals, moving, and breathing in the fresh air can do wonders for your body. It's a great chance to free your mind of everything. It can be as simple as going outside in your own backyard or taking a hike in a state park.

- Be Mindful

You can't control what happened in your past. What happens in every moment is what controls the future, so you need to be focused on what is happening right now. Stop constantly worrying about what you did last month or last year. Stop worrying about what you might be in the future. You have to focus on the right now and right here. You have to choose to be present and be your best self each moment and each day.

- Your Living Space

Your environment has lasting impacts on your happiness and mood. Is there clutter in your room? Is the color on your walls something you hate? Do thoughts clutter your mind?

If you answered yes to any of these questions, it just might be time for a makeover. Putting a fresh coat of paint on your walls and rearranging your furniture can do wonders. Find a fragranced candle that you love the smell of that makes you happy. Fill your surroundings with things that show the real you. These things need to bring you joy and make you feel proud.

- It's Okay To Say No

Nobody can be a yes man all the time. You can't get anything out of a cup that is empty. It takes a lot of guts and strength to say no to somebody if you don't want to do what they asked, but it will make you happy. Reserve your energy and time for all the other things in life that make you happy. Stop wasting them on trying to impress people who don't matter.

- Express Yourself

Today, more than ever, it is important for you to express yourself. You have to be the person you want to be. Go out and find some new clothes at your local thrift store or dye your hair a cool color. Start a hobby that you have always wanted to try. When you can really express who you are and stop caring what other people think about you, it will be a freeing experience that will bring you wonderful amounts of joy.

- Decide When to Receive and Give

Giving is the main thing that can bring you joy. Giving to other people what you are able to can work wonders. These things don't have to be physical. Give someone some kind words, your talent, and time. You also need to decide when you want to receive it because you matter.

If people would like to give you presents, you deserve them. Just remember to be grateful for all the things you have and the things you receive, and you will be truly happy.

Happiness is a choice. It won't ever be anything instant. It is going to take some time to develop the right attitude to choose to be happy even during the most trying situations.

This doesn't mean happiness isn't possible. Please note that deciding to be happy can be hard at times. People who have mental problems might have a hard time being happy.

Everybody can be happy to a certain degree daily. You just need to begin small and create new habits with time. Understand that being happy doesn't have to be constant. It's important to experience every emotion, and this includes all the negative ones. This means that when you finally experience happiness, it will be worth it a lot more.

AFTERWORD

Thank you for making it through to the end of *Minimalist Living*, let's hope it was informative and able to provide you with all of the tools you need to achieve your goals whatever they may be.

The next step is to start using the information we have gone over. Not everybody will mesh with a minimalist lifestyle, and that's okay. I'm guessing, though, that since you read all the way through the book, there are aspects of this lifestyle that you find intriguing. Go forth and use those tips and tricks to bring more balance into your life. Remove the physical and mental clutter from your life, and notice what happens. You'll be amazed at how amazing your life can be.

Finally, if you found this book useful in any way, a review is always appreciated!

Thank you in advance.